LIFE IS RELIGION

12 DAILY EXERCISES FOR MIND, BODY, AND SOUL

BOOKS BY LAURA KNIGHT-JADCZYK

The Secret History of the World
The Noah Syndrome
High Strangeness: Hyperdimensions and the Process of Alien Abduction
9/11: The Ultimate Truth
The Apocalypse: Comets, Asteroids and Cyclical Catastrophes
Amazing Grace

THE WAVE SERIES:

Riding the Wave
Soul Hackers
The Terror of History
Stripped to the Bone
Petty Tyrants
Facing the Unknown
Almost Human
Debugging the Universe

LIFE IS RELIGION

12 DAILY EXERCISES FOR MIND, BODY, AND SOUL

Written and compiled by the Quantum Future Group
discussion forum at Cassiopaea.org

Red Pill Press
www.redpillpress.com

CONTENTS

1. Growth in Knowledge   7

2. Cleansing the Heart with Éiriú Eolas   11

3. Assimilating Knowledge and Being   16

4. Staying Vigilant About Diet   19

5. Protecting Psychic Hygiene   22

6. Pure Faith and Non-Anticipation   25

7. Staying Vigilant Against Psychic Attacks   28

8. Self-Remember, Self-Observe   33

9. Paying Strict Attention to Objective Reality
   Left and Right   36

10. Have the Will of a Lion   39

11. Discerning Emotions   43

12. Network, Network, Network!   47

Expanded Glossary and Definitions   55

     Anticipation and non-Anticipation   56
     Laura Knight-Jadczyk, *The Wave*, Chapter 23 (excerpt)   58
     The Cassiopaean Experiment   64
     External and Internal Considering   67
     Networking   70
     Paleo Diet Summary   72
     Recapitulation   75
     Self-Remembering   76
     Strategic Enclosure   77
     The Wave   81

Recommended Reading   85

Notes   87

*"There are periods in the life of humanity, which generally
coincide with the beginning of the fall of cultures and
civilizations, when the masses irretrievably lose their reason
and begin to destroy everything that has been created by
centuries and millenniums of culture. Such periods of mass
madness, often coinciding with geological cataclysms, climatic
changes, and similar phenomena of a planetary character,
release a very great quantity of the matter of knowledge.
This, in its turn, necessitates the work of collecting this matter
of knowledge, which would otherwise be lost.
Thus the work of collecting scattered matter of knowledge
frequently coincides with the beginning of the destruction
and fall of cultures and civilizations."*

—*G. I. Gurdjieff, in P. D. Ouspensky's*
In Search of the Miraculous.

Growth in Knowledge

Make a dedicated effort every day to increase your knowledge about yourself and the world. Whether through books, movies, or simply observing the world around you and the people in it with purposeful attention, you can catch glimpses of truth. No topic is off limits when it comes to searching for truth, so follow your curiosity: science, history, philosophy, psychology, religion. But think critically.

Knowledge protects against all forms of misfortune and shows the way toward new possibilities. When you know the possible harms, you can take steps to be prepared. And by gaining knowledge, one learns to discern between illusion and truth, the petty concerns of everyday existence and the things that really matter, like self-work and seeing reality as it is. At the end of every day, ask yourself, what have I learned today? 'An idle mind is the devil's playground.'

Quotations

Q: (L) What can be done for shielding [from harmful influences]?

A: Knowledge input on a continuous basis.

—*The Cassiopaeans (15 April 1995)*

"Remember the most important principles the Cassiopaeans have given us: free will, and knowledge protects. These two concepts are inseparable. The more knowledge you have, the more awareness you have; and the more awareness you have, the more free will you have."

—*Laura Knight-Jadczyk*, The Wave *(Chapter 71)*

Q: (L) I don't understand. How can knowledge help to cancel programming?

A: So that the awareness can be the foundation for being able to deal with situations, and possibly rectify some of them.

—*The Cassiopaeans (12 October 1996)*

"In this factitious life, ruled by Illusion, yet strewn with 'B' influences, we must reaffirm our values almost every day if we are not to fall into another trap. We generally agree to recognize the existence of the danger of Illusion, but rather theoretically; most often, we see its action on those round about us, but not on ourselves. **We continue to live day by day in the same old way, so that the power we know as the Devil still triumphs. Whatever name we give it, it remains ever-present. We live in an artificial, illusory world.** It is interesting in this context to quote the words of a Buddhist monk. Asked: 'How do you describe the creation of the world?', he answered: 'The world is created anew for each new-born person.' This is exact. **The power of illusion which chains us exerts its action individually on each one of us, as well as collectively.** Each mind is falsified in a way peculiar to it. What can be the outcome of such a situation? If we keep quietly to our place, human careers open to us ... just as long as we stay far away from the void. We may have a happy or unhappy life; a family life; a life of loves; we may make discoveries, travel, write. Then comes the end.

"Our reasoning starts to become more realistic if our attention is concentrated on this end. Everything can happen to us in life; or nothing. Our aspirations can be fulfilled or unfulfilled, but there is a sure end, which is death. ...

"Constatation can take various forms, appropriate to the chosen object and attitude. But doubled attention is always obligatory. The exercise of presence is an effort of watchfulness; as we have seen, it is the principal element in this. **When done daily, in the**

form of passive constatation, it leads to knowledge of oneself.
But because presence must as far as possible become permanent—
and we emphasize this point because of its importance—the seeker
must practise doubled attention as much as he can during all his
activities. He will notice in time that this effort of memory, of pres-
ence, not only does not hinder his activities, but on the contrary
it helps greatly in carrying them out."

—*Boris Mouravieff,* Gnosis *(Vol. 1, pp. 143, 212)*

Cleansing the Heart with Éiriú Eolas

The principal aim of self-work is the development of emotions. The **Éiriú Eolas** breathing and meditation program not only relieves stress, but also releases repressed emotions and increases one's awareness of their own body, emotions, and thoughts. These are all essential steps in preparing oneself to truly assimilate knowledge and grow spiritually. (Deep-tissue bodywork can also be effective.)

The Wave will bring a hyperkinetic sensate and all feelings will be felt. Cases of pathology, like psychotic episodes and drug-induced visions, can open one to other levels of reality that are overwhelming and for which body and mind are not prepared. A macrocosmic shift in realities like the Wave will be much more potent, bringing up repressed emotions in full force. Daily practice of Éiriú Eolas is therefore essential for releasing whatever potentially harmful emotions are hidden and repressed below the threshold of consciousness, and for gaining the ability to experience stronger and stronger emotions, without traumatizing oneself.

Quotations

Q: (L) Okay, so now you say that we have taken steps towards joy. The joy of a new world.

A: The wave is coming, you are teaching people to surf it instead of being dragged under and out to stormy seas.

Q: (L) You once said that the wave was something like "hyperkinetic sensate." And I've often wondered if that means that it's something that massively amplifies whatever is inside an individual? And if that were the case and they were full of a lot of unpleasant, painful, miserable feelings, repressed and suppressed thoughts and so forth, and something that was hyperkinetic sensate amplified all of that, what would it do to that individual? I mean, can you imagine any of us in our worst state of feeling yucky and then having that amplified a bazillion times? If it was bad stuff inside you, you would implode!

A: Soul smashing!

Q: (L) So it is really important for people to go through this process of cleansing to prepare themselves for that?

A: Yes, then they will "rise up with wings as eagles"!

Q: (L) So even people who—or maybe particularly people who — engage in a great deal of what Lobaczewski called "selection and substitution", there is some part of their rational mind that knows what the truth is, but because it's not acceptable to their peer group, or their social milieu, or their background and upbringing to accept that truth, they repress and suppress it and explain things to themselves in other ways. But they still know the truth. What would it be like if you have all of this suppressed, twisted truth locked up inside you that you never allowed yourself to look at and acknowledge? (A) But you see this is not a separate phenomenon because when there is this amplification, there are these fears that you said, they will also explode. So the individual will be able to ... the little devil will become the big devil, so it will be easier to choose, because, you know, choices will be amplified. It's not just little dark here, little this there—it's hard to choose —but they will have to decide this time where to go, and the decision will be ... (L) Extremely painful. (A) It will be painful, but on the other hand, it will be clear. (C) But what if you're so overwhelmed it isn't clear? (L) What if your fear is so big that ... (C) You're blinded? (A) Well, then you are lost.

—*The Cassiopaeans (28 November 2009)*

"*Among the lower centres, the emotional centre is worst off. In our civilization—as we have already observed—generally receives neither rational education nor systematic training. **Its formation***

and development are now left to chance, *since religious education today has been largely intellectualized and rationalized. All sorts of considerations dictated by worldly wisdom and mundane vanity; the habitual practice of lying—especially to ourselves—and hypocrisy, from which no one is totally exempt,* **imprint dangerous distortions on the emotional centre**. *Frequently struck by a feeling of inferiority and by the need for compensation, its usual motivation; accustomed as it is to judge and to criticize everybody and everything; surrendering itself to a strangely voluptuous enjoyment of negative emotions; this centre becomes unrecognizable.* **It degenerates to the point where it becomes the instrument of destruction of our being**, *which it accelerates on its way towards ageing and death."*

—*Boris Mouravieff,* Gnosis *(Vol. 1, pp. 45–6)*

Q: (C) [Éiriú Eolas] serves to help people who don't know how to control their mind or their emotions.

A: Yes. And teach them when where and how to use those emotions for change. Overcoming emotions so that one is not affected by what is out there and inside is little more than becoming an automaton.

—*The Cassiopaeans (7 March 2009)*

"I was thinking that emotions could, at a stretch, be likened a little to an internal traffic light. If this light is working properly it is an essential tool to navigate this reality correctly. But for most people their 'traffic light' is all messed up, all the wiring is partially burned out or crossed. Wrong lights go off at the wrong time, sometimes the green shows when the red should, etc., and sometimes they all flash in chaos together. This naturally causes a lot of problems for the person who tries to rely on it for navigation.

Two solutions seem possible: either turn off the traffic light alto-gether (or find a way to ignore it) **or recalibrate it so that it runs correctly and gives accurate signals.**

"These breathing techniques can apparently be useful in shutting off the chaotic working of the lights, but that is not enough because they must be recalibrated. What is needed is for the traffic light to receive accurate data input in order to then begin working in the right way, **and that's where knowledge input comes in.**"

—*Perceval (Cassiopaea Forum Moderator)*

Assimilating Knowledge and Being

Aside from the effort involved in doing them, exercises 1 and 2 are relatively passive. Reading books will increase the general knowledge at your disposal, and meditation will help initiate processes that heal the soul and emotions. But for these to have any real effect—for real *learning* and understanding to take place—you need to make active efforts to work on the self and apply your knowledge directly. The ability to assimilate knowledge is directly tied to your level of being, and being is who you truly are, your emotional nature.

The more you learn, the more you can apply. And the more you apply, the more you can learn. But if you make no attempt to work though psychological buffers, rationalizations, prejudices and lies, then your level of being is stopped in its growth. It's most likely the emotional centre that will suffer from these psychological defects, and higher knowledge won't be accessible. So lies to the self must be identified and stopped immediately. The recommended books dealing with narcissism and the adaptive unconscious can help reveal these issues.

Quotations

"All there is is lessons. This is one infinite school."
—The Cassiopaeans (24 November 1994)

"Simple ideas are the most difficult to grasp. They escape us because the extreme complexity of our minds makes us complicate everything. It is only simple ideas and formula: that matter in life.

"Let us now consider the relation between these notions: to know, and to understand.

"We can know without understanding, but we cannot understand without knowing. It therefore follows that understanding is knowing to which something imponderable is added. We are touching on a problem which is simple but at the same time can raise great difficulties.

*"We pass from knowing to understanding to the measure that we assimilate knowledge. **The capacity for assimilation has its limits: man's capacity to contain understanding differs from person to person.***

"This problem concerns what we call the being of a person. It is one of the basic notions of esoteric science. It has several facets. In the terms that concern us here, being is demonstrated by a person's capacity for assimilation.

"Knowledge is widespread everywhere. However, it is external to us. Understanding is within us.

"If we pour the contents of a bottle into a glass, the latter can only contain an amount equal to its capacity. Any more will overflow. That is exactly what happens with us. We are only capable of understanding within the limits of our capacity to contain understanding within our being.

"Jesus said to His disciples: 'I have yet many things to say unto you but ye cannot contain them now.'

"To be able to evolve, in the esoteric sense of the term, we must above everything else constantly seek to enhance our being, to raise its level."

—*Boris Mouravieff,* Gnosis *(Vol. 1, p. 12)*

"In fact, in terms of our reality, each and every source of information has its place and purpose. Everyone who is seeking is at some point on the learning cycle. The old saying, 'When the student is ready, the teacher will appear,' is appropriate in this respect. It would do no good for a child in second grade to work with a teacher who specializes in sixth grade material ——he or she simply would gain nothing from the interaction but confusion."

—*Laura Knight-Jadczyk,* The Wave *(Chapter 10)*

Staying vigilant about Diet

Your body is the only one you have, so take care of it! But before you do, do plenty of research and make sure you gain the knowledge to do it right. The human diet has been getting progressively worse ever since the invention of agriculture, and especially so in recent years, with refined sugars, GMOs, vegetable oils, chemical additives, and grain-fed meats. And as our diet has deviated from our ideal, so has our health. The modern 'high-carb, low-fat' diet contributes to countless diseases of body and mind. If you want to use the full potentials of your body and mind, you need to give it the fuel it was designed to burn: animal fats. That means a 'very-low-carb, high-fat' ketogenic (or '**Paleo**') diet.

Food is fuel for your body, which you need to think clearly and make good choices. While food can and should be satisfying, a well-oiled machine trumps a brain-frying sugar-fest. The real goal is to be able to Work. Don't obsess about health, however. You can't avoid all toxins, but you can take preventative measures with your diet to mitigate the harmful effects. Remember Pavlov's dogs.

Quotations

"First Striving: To have in [your] ordinary being-existence every-thing satisfying and really necessary for [your] planetary body."
— G. I. Gurdjieff, Beelzebub's Tales to His Grandson.

Q: (L) The first question is: "Do genetically modified foods affect human DNA?"

A: Yes! Very bad.

Q: (L) Okay. What are the consequences of this disruption in terms of awareness and spiritual growth?

A: Remember Pavlov?

Q: (L) Yeah ... So what about Pavlov?

A: Strong dogs can be broken if their health is broken first.

Q: (L) So you're saying that these effects are primarily health-related?

A: Yes.

Q: (L) So if your health is compromised, it makes it more difficult for you to achieve any kind of awareness or spiritual growth. Is that it?

A: Yes. Hasn't that always been the case?
— The Cassiopaeans (28 March 2010)

Q: (L) But I would say that just the eating of meat is not a spiritual issue at all. (Perceval) Eating food is a thing of the body. (L) Yeah, I mean we just try to eat in an optimal way to give our bodies the right fuel so that we can do our other work. That's our whole thing is to give the body optimal fuel.

A: There is the difference, see? You eat for optimal fuel, they eat to support an illusion.

Q: (L) Well, they don't all eat to support an illusion. A lot of them

20

think that vegetables are an optimal fuel illusion. (Perceval) But they couldn't think that if they really objectively read all the details.

A: They lack objective knowledge.

—The Cassiopaeans (11 June 2011)

A: When humankind "fell" into gross matter, a way was needed to return. This way simply is a manifestation of the natural laws. Consciousness must "eat" also. This is a natural function of the life giving nature of the environment in balance. The Earth is the Great Mother who gives her body, literally, in the form of creatures with a certain level of consciousness for the sustenance of her children of the cosmos. This is the original meaning of those sayings.

Q: (L) So, eating flesh also means eating consciousness which accumulates, I'm assuming is what is being implied here, or what feeds our consciousness so that it grows in step with our bodies? Is that close?

A: Close enough.

Q: (Ailen) And when you eat veggies you're basically eating a much lower level of consciousness. (L) Not only that, but in a sense you're rejecting the gift and you're not feeding consciousness. And that means that all eating of meat should be a sacrament.

A: Yes

—The Cassiopaeans (20 August 2011)

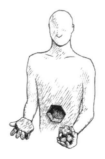

21

Protecting Psychic Hygiene

Just as a bad diet can hinder self-work, so can your psychic hygiene. Are you listening to negative music, watching mind-numbing television, or in general surrounding yourself with negativity without calling it negative? That's lying to yourself. Call a spade a spade.

If you like a movie, but it is full of propaganda, admit it to yourself. If you like a writer, but know that he has a questionable or pathological character, don't make excuses for him. Recognize each influence in your life for what it is, without the rose-tinted glasses.

Quotations

Q: (L) The first one is: why have we all been feeling so inflamed/low on energy/depressed/irritable for the last two weeks?

A: Cosmic changes in process. Each person experiences this differently according to genetics and environment. Recall previous sufferings preparatory to DNA boosts? All must keep vigilant about diet and psychic hygiene during this time as there are also external factors that seek to block the natural process. …

Q: (Burma Jones) What do they mean by "psychic hygiene"?

A: Being careful about what you allow into your "field".

Q: (L) In what sense?

A: All senses.

Q: (L) What do you mean "all senses"?

A: Seeing, hearing, speaking, and so on …

A: Take care with interacting with negative energies.

Q: (L) Well that's kinda like creating your own reality, isn't it?

A: Not what we mean … Keep your guard up and do not allow negative energies to slip by … such as believing lies … listening to negative music while thinking it is positive … watching negative movies and thinking it is negligible. It is extremely important to not lie to the self. **One can listen or watch many things as long as the truth of the orientation is known, acknowledged, and understood.** *Clear?*

Q: (L) So, in other words: awareness. Calling a spade a spade and not allowing something negative to enter you and believing

it is positive. You can see it, perceive it and acknowledge it but not allow it to influence you. **Because obviously, you cannot shut off your perceptions of the world, but you can control how it affects you.** *So, don't let it inside, thinking it's something that it's not. (Belibaste) So, see it as it is. If it is negative, see it as negative. (L) Yeah, and they're saying to focus on truth in order for changes to manifest in you that are positive. That is, "positive" can mean acknowledging that something is negative because it is truth.*

Q: (Galatea) Choose the seeds you wish to water. (L) Is that basically what we're talking about here?

A: Yes.

—The Cassiopaeans (9 April 2011)

Pure Faith and Non-Anticipation

In your everyday plans and actions, use pure faith and mental denial (**non-anticipation**). When you set a goal and work towards achieving it, having too rigid a mindset can block the process. Sometimes new opportunities or unanticipated alternatives will come up. Sometimes the solution to a problem will present itself in a way that you couldn't have expected. But if you're too fearful and rigid in your outlook, you might miss the signs that will lead you toward your goal. Why anticipate anything? Focus on today. Be aware today.

What is faith? A good description is from *The Sufi Path of Knowledge*: the basic meaning is, to be or feel safe and secure concerning your knowledge of God, i.e., the totality of existence, and to commit yourself to putting this into practice. It is speaking, and doing from the heart (higher emotional center), based on knowledge. It is striving to be your true self and acting according to the Cosmic Mind living within us, with full trust in the wisdom of the cosmos that is impersonal and not self-interested. In short, it is *trusting the process*.

Quotations

"Live as if you were to die tomorrow. Learn as if you were to live forever."

—*Mahatma Ghandi*

"Of course, we see that completely pure intent is a pretty tall order. Thus we see that the key becomes acting now with intent, but no imaginary anticipation for the future. A goal, with applied will of action, which necessitates left brain conscious preparing and planning, via the heightened awareness of the right brain, which deals directly with the present conditions, will result in an opening of life changing creative potential."

—*Laura Knight-Jadczyk,* The Wave *(Chapter 23)*

Q: (L) If someone wanted to win the lottery, for example, what would be the correct approach? What should they do, or be, or think, or say?

A: Completely pure intent, i.e., open. Nonanticipatory.

Q: (L) Anticipation constricts the channels of creativity?

A: Yes.

Q: (L) A person has to be completely uncaring whether they get it or not, so to speak?

A: Happy-go-lucky attitude helps.

Q: (L) So, worry, tension, anticipation, and attachment to the idea constrict the flow?

A: Yes.

—*The Cassiopaeans (9 December 1994)*

Staying Vigilant Against Psychic Attacks

Psyche means soul or mind in Greek. The soul is the subconscious mind. Now think of how many ways we are affected subconsciously, from literally everything: advertising, newspapers, movies, music, social interactions, tradition. These are the 'A influences' that trap us in everyday life, and they can be used malevolently to keep us from discovering the truth. Propaganda can be used by people in power to tap our emotions, instilled hopelessness can lead to suicidal thoughts, and peer pressure can prevent us from doing what is right. Knowledge protects, and self-knowledge is key here.

Don't underestimate the opposition to becoming free. Just as in *The Matrix*, the forces that wish to keep you asleep can work through strangers, friends, and family who may have your best interests at heart. So watch what you say and do to avoid the general law assault. This means practicing **external considering** and non-internal considering, developing a **strategic enclosure** in which you can work on yourself without external hindrances. Sun Tzu wrote: "If you know the enemy and know yourself you need not fear the results of a hundred battles." The battle is always being fought through us: our own self-importance, lack of consideration for others, and lack of knowledge.

Quotations

Q: (L) Well, when one is dealing with psychology, what would be the best approach … what is the true aspect of the self or the being that one should inquire into in order to heal?

A: Subconscious mind.

Q: (V) Is the statement that psychology studies emotions, is that a fair statement?

A: No. Subconscious is same in body or out.

Q: (V) The subconscious is part of the soul?

A: One and same.

Q: (V) Is the higher self the same as the soul and the subconscious?

A: Yes. —The Cassiopaeans (23 December 1994)

"The Matrix is a system, Neo. That system is our enemy. But when you're inside, you look around, what do you see? Businessmen, teachers, lawyers, carpenters. The very minds of the people we are trying to save. But until we do, these people are still a part of that system and that makes them our enemy. You have to understand, most of these people are not ready to be unplugged. And many of them are so inured, so hopelessly dependent on the system, that they will fight to protect it."

—The Matrix

"The conflict between the need to be accurate and the desire to feel good about ourselves is one of the major battlegrounds of the

29

self, and how this battle is waged and how it is won are central determinants of who we are and how we feel about ourselves."
—*Timothy Wilson,* Strangers to Ourselves *(p. 39)*

"For instance, I am sitting here, and although I am used to sitting with my legs crossed under me, I consider the opinion of those present, what they are accustomed to, and I sit as they do, with legs down. Now someone gives me a disapproving look. This immediately starts corresponding associations in my feeling, and I am annoyed. I am too weak to refrain from reacting, from considering internally. ... Usually we live like that; what we feel inside we manifest outside. But a boundary line should be established between the inner and the outer, and one should learn to refrain from reacting inwardly to anything, not to consider outer impacts, but externally sometimes to consider more than we do now. For instance, when we have to be polite, we should if necessary learn to be even more polite than we have been till now."
—*G. I. Gurdjieff,* Views from the Real World *(pp. 256–7)*

"The opposite of internal considering and what is in part a means of fighting against it is external considering.

External considering is based upon an entirely different relationship towards people, to their understanding, to their requirements. By considering externally a man does that which makes life easy for other people and for himself.

External considering requires a knowledge of men, an understanding of their tastes, habits, and prejudices. At the same time external considering requires a great power over oneself, a great control over oneself.

Very often a man desires sincerely to express or somehow or other show to another man what he really thinks of him or feels about him. And if he is a weak man he will of course give way to this desire and afterwards justify himself and say that he did not want to lie, did not want to pretend, he wanted to be sincere. Then he convinces himself that it was the other man's fault. He really wanted to consider him, even to give way to him, not to quarrel, and so on. But the other man did not at all want to consider him so that nothing could be done with him.

It very often happens that a man begins with a blessing and ends with a curse. He begins by deciding not to consider and afterwards blames other people for not considering him.

This is an example of how external considering passes into internal considering. But if a man really remembers himself he understands that another man is a machine just as he is himself. And then he will enter into his position, he will put himself in his place, and he will be really able to understand and feel what another man thinks and feels.

If he can do this his work becomes easier for him. But if he ap-

proaches a man with his own requirements nothing except new internal considering can ever be obtained from it."
—*G. I. Gurdjieff, in P. D. Ouspensky's*
In Search of the Miraculous *(p. 153)*

"A man's enemies will be the members of his own household."
—*Matthew 10:36*

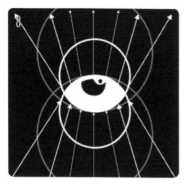

Self-Remember, Self-Observe

Practice **self-remembering** and self-observation. Essentially, self-remembering is being aware that you are aware, and self-observation is observing your body, emotions, and thoughts. Self-observation helps you gain knowledge of yourself: how you react to certain situations, your unconscious habits, and the things you waste energy on. A key to observing the self is to turn the attention simultaneously towards others to notice their true reactions to what you think you are doing or how you think you are being perceived. In other words, making the unconscious conscious. **Recapitulation** is useful in freeing yourself from your past through bringing it to consciousness, seeing where you have succeeded and failed. Accept the past and the present without resistance and wishing things to be different. Focus on learning from the past and present to prepare for the future.

By being mindful of yourself in every situation, you act consciously instead of just reacting or 'forgetting yourself' and doing something you'll later regret. Being aware allows you to practice external consideration, so you can navigate situations competently and appropriately. It allows you to really apply everything you have learned in your everyday life. Applying your knowledge generates energy, allowing you to do even more.

Quotations

Q: And utilization [of knowledge] means ...
A: Knowledge application which generates energy, which, in turn, generates light.
                              —*The Cassiopaeans (31 May 1997)*

"There are moments when you become aware not only of what you are doing but also of yourself doing it. You see both 'I' and the 'here' of 'I am here'—both the anger and the 'I' that is angry. Call this self-remembering if you like."
                    —*G. I. Gurdjieff,* Views From the Real World

"Paradoxically, the only way that we can know ourselves is in learning to be mindfully aware of the moment-to-moment goings-on of our body and mind as they exist through various situations occurring in time. We have no experience of anything that is permanent and independent of this."
                    —*Peter Levine,* In An Unspoken Voice *(p. 287)*

"[A]wareness is the spontaneous, and creatively neutral, experiencing of whatever arises in the present moment—whether sensation, feeling, perception, thought or action. ... 'simple' awareness, along with a fortified tolerance for bewildering and frightening physical body sensations, can seemingly, as if by magic, prevent or dissolve entrenched emotional and physical symptoms."
              —*Peter Levine,* In An Unspoken Voice *(pp. 289-290)*

"*Try for a moment to accept the idea that you are not what you believe yourself to be, that you overestimate yourself, in fact that you lie to yourself. That you always lie to yourself every moment, all day, all your life. That this lying rules you to such an extent that you cannot control it any more. You are the prey of lying. You lie, everywhere. Your relations with others—lies. The upbringing you give, the conventions—lies. Your teaching—lies. Your theories, your art- lies. Your social life, your family life—lies. And what you think of yourself—lies also.*

"*But you never stop yourself in what you are doing or in what you are saying because you believe in yourself. You must stop inwardly and observe. Observe without preconceptions, accepting for a time this idea of lying. And if you observe in this way, paying with yourself, without self-pity, giving up all your supposed riches for a moment of reality, perhaps you will suddenly see something you have never before seen in yourself until this day.*

"*You will see that you are different from what you think you are.*"

—*Uncertain (G. I. Gurdjieff or Jeanne de Salzmann),*
'The First Initiation'

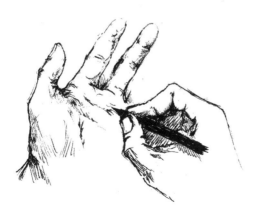

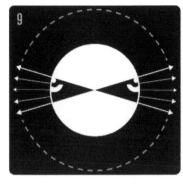

Paying Strict Attention to Objective Reality Left and Right

'Awareness' means having or showing realization, perception, or knowledge and in archaic terms means being watchful and wary. Do you know what is going on in the world? Are you watching and reading the signs and changes in our reality? Being aware of the world around you is just as important as being aware of your own self. Don't ignore current events! Stay up to date and watch the signs, because you can't do spiritual work without knowing what's going on in the world around you.

In fact, the essence of spiritual work is learning the truth about yourself and the world around you. And the truth is that we live in a prison. Living a life in isolation from the general state of the world is a denial of truth, and decidedly un-spiritual. The propagandistic nature of current news publications and broadcasts can be disconcerting. Luckily, alternative news websites like SOTT.net work to present current events and insightful analysis with truth as their guiding purpose.

Quotations

"Life is religion. Life experiences reflect how one interacts with God. Those who are asleep are those of little faith in terms of their interaction with the creation. Some people think that the world exists for them to overcome or ignore or shut out. For those individuals, the world will cease. They will become exactly what they give to life. They will become merely a dream in the 'past.' People who pay strict attention to objective reality right and left, become the reality of the 'Future.'"

—*The Cassiopaeans (28 September 2002)*

"It is generally admitted that the effect of the Delphian oracle upon Greek culture was profoundly constructive. James Gardner sums up its influence in the following words: **"Its responses re-**

*vealed many a tyrant and foretold his fate. Through its means many an unhappy being was saved from destruction and many a perplexed mortal guided in the right way. It encouraged useful institutions, and promoted the progress of useful discoveries. **Its moral influence was on the side of virtue, and its political influence in favor of the advancement of civil liberty.**"*

—*Manly P. Hall,* The Secret Teachings of All Ages

Q: (L) I have a question I want to ask. A lot of people say that esotericism and politics shouldn't be mixed together, that somebody who has esoteric pursuits—or spiritual pursuits, let me put it that way—shouldn't be interested in 'worldly' things. I would like to have your view on this. Have we gone completely astray by mixing in politics?

*A: Absolutely and vehemently not!!! **There is no possibility of true spiritual work progressing without full awareness of the world that surrounds you.** What have we said about "true religion?" Let your curiosity guide you. In its pure state curiosity is a spiritual function.*

—*The Cassiopaeans (2 January 2009)*

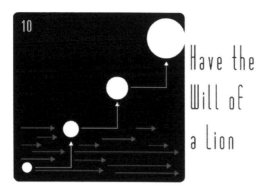

Have the Will of a Lion

Humans are creatures of habit, and we often find ourselves in situations over which we have little choice. We live under the threat of events beyond our power to control, like natural disasters or political violence. Corporations and politicians require our complacence and often have hidden or harmful agendas, and we don't want to be a part of them. It's hard to overcome the inertia of just reacting passively to the world around us, like turning on the TV when we could be doing something worthwhile. We procrastinate, and this keeps us from seeing and doing. Either we use energy for learning or lose energy by escaping. But this doesn't mean that you are powerless. You have free will, so use it.

Give yourself daily will-tasks. Set a goal and follow it through, no matter how small or trivial. The only way to build willpower is to start small. So when you promise to do something, do it. Build from there to bigger tasks. Keeping a daily goal in mind may keep you from falling into a state of procrastination. Today is the day, not tomorrow. Practice voluntary discomfort periodically. This has the benefit of hardening the spirit for any future misfortune, building willpower and confidence, and helping with the realization that we can make do with less than what we use today. You have a will, therefore you may choose now to prepare for whatever changes the future may bring.

Quotations

A: *"If one has the will of a Lion, one does not have the fate of a mouse!"* Arkadiusz is strong willed. Must be to be seeker of worlds. To paraphrase: *"I am become ONE … Creator of worlds."*

—The Cassiopaeans (12 July 1997)

"Act as if the fate of the universe depends on your actions, even in the most trivial of situations."

—Arkadiusz Jadczyk

"This strange disease 'tomorrow' brought with it terrifying con-sequences, and particularly for those unfortunate [humans] there who chance to learn and to become categorically convinced with the whole of their presence that they possess some very undesirable consequences for the deliverance from which they must make cer-tain efforts, and which efforts moreover they even know just how to make, **but owing to this maleficent disease 'tomorrow' they never succeed in making these required efforts.** *...*

"Thanks to the disease 'tomorrow,' the three-brained beings there, particularly the contemporary ones, almost always put off till 'later' everything that needs to be done at the moment, being convinced that 'later' they will do better and more."

—*G. I. Gurdjieff,* Beelzebub's Tales to His Grandson

"The way in which man accepts his fate and all the suffering it entails, the way in which he takes up his cross, gives him ample opportunity—even under the most difficult circumstances—to add a deeper meaning to his life. It may remain brave, dignified, and unselfish. Or in the bitter fight for self-preservation he may forget his human dignity and become no more than an animal. Here lies the chance for a man either to make use of or to forego the op-portunities of attaining the moral values that a difficult situation may afford him. And this decides whether he is worthy of his suf-ferings or not."

—*Viktor Frankl,* Man's Search for Meaning

"Impeccability is nothing else but the proper use of energy," he said. *"My statements have no inkling of morality. I've saved energy and that makes me impeccable. To understand this, you have to save enough energy yourself."*

"Warriors take strategic inventories," he said. *"They list every-thing they do. Then they decide which of those things can be changed in order to allow themselves a respite, in terms of ex-pending their energy."*

—*Carlos Castaneda,* The Fire From Within

Discerning Emotions

We're driven by our emotions. This is what makes us so easy to manipulate. Following inflictions of narcissistic wounding and other trauma there will often be the loss of a felt sense, the detachment from body awareness, making emotional reactions even more distant or intangible. Unfortunately, because of a lack of proper emotional education, most people also tend to live relatively limited and stunted emotional lives. We desire to feel this limited range of passions to feel alive and avoid death. But emotions are more than just feel-good drugs: they're the key to our self-development. We're left with having to correctly identify and control our emotions, not letting them rule us, but listening to what they tell us. Fear can be a lifesaver, and anger can fuel conscious action.

Use active reasoning to deal with negative emotions. For example: When someone insults you, ask yourself if it was justified. If yes, accept it and do better in the future. If not justified, consider that the other has made a mistake and stop bothering about it. Uncouple sensation from thought and feeling. For example:

When angry, focus on your breath, posture and tension in the body instead of letting the energy drive imaginary thoughts. Try to catch the anger before it passes the level of the neck. End each day by asking: What ailment of yours have you cured today? What failing have you resisted? Where can you show improvement?

Quotations

"Although education is a major preoccupation of families and public authorities, the emotional development of the child is almost totally left to chance. In our contemporary civilization, this leads to an extraordinary impoverishment of our affective lives. Even in the eighteenth century, the Abbe Prevost notes:

"'There are few people who know the full force of the different movements of the heart. The vast majority of men are only sensitive to five or six passions, in the circle of which their lives are passed and which define the boundaries of their imaginations. Take away

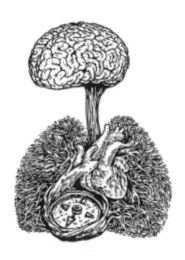

love and hate, pleasure and pain, hope and fear, and they will feel nothing.'

"He further added:

"'But persons of a nobler character can be moved in thousands of different ways. It seems that they can receive ideas and sensations which surpass the ordinary norms of nature.'

"The development of the emotional centre is the principal object of esoteric culture. We shall see later that it is only through this centre that man can find the key which will open the door to give him access to a higher life."

—Boris Mouravieff, Gnosis (Vol. 1, pp. 33–4)

"Emotional reactivity almost always precludes conscious awareness. On the other hand, restraint and containment of expressive impulse allows us to become aware of our underlying postural attitude. Therefore it is the restraint that brings a feeling into conscious awareness. Change only occurs when there is mindfulness and mindfulness only occurs where there is bodily feeling (i.e., awareness of the postural attitude). ... The uncoupling of sensation from image and thought is what diffuses the highly charged emotions and allows them to transform fluidly into sensation-based gradations of feelings. This is not at all the same as suppressing or repressing them."

—Peter Levine, In An Unspoken Voice (pp. 338, 322)

"Okay, now picture yourself in a forest clearing. In that clearing you are surrounded by a pack of wolves. These wolves, in your mind, represent a blockage. The blockage is emotion. Emotion is a necessary component of life in 3rd density. It can be of great assistance, and it can also be a hindrance. Normally, in critical situations closest to the 3rd density individual's existence, these emotions serve temporarily as hindrances. So, we ask you to picture these wolves surrounding you. And, as wolves will do when addressed in a calm voice, when one takes a deep breath internally and externally, and asks the wolves in a calming, reassuring voice, to simply go back into the forest, that all is well, then the wolves turn and retreat, as wolves will do. This removes the hindering aspect of emotion, which allows intuition to become stronger. Then, in turn, one's intuitions are not 'torn.'"

—*The Cassiopaeans (7 October 1997)*

"*Emotion that limits is an impediment to progress. Emotion is also necessary to make progress in 3rd density. It is natural.* **When you begin to separate limiting emotions based on assumptions from emotions that open one to unlimited possibilities, that means you are preparing for the next density.**"

—*The Cassiopaeans (9 September 1995)*

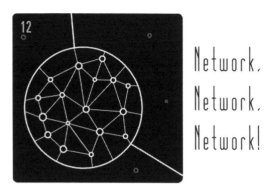

Network, Network, Network!

No one person can have a complete understanding of everything, especially of themselves. We all have our particular insights and talents. We simply cannot work alone; we need a network of like-minded individuals heading in the same direction, able to share their unique points of view and point out the things we cannot see in ourselves. A true network is a community geared towards soul growth. By networking with others, we are connecting on a soul level that extends far beyond the material plane. This work can literally change the world for the better so be persistent and let things happen naturally.

Read, share insights, experience, articles, and help uplift others. You will also begin to see yourself though mirrors and any errors you have will be revealed to you. In other words, your own behaviors and character will be reflected back to you, to help you see what you cannot see in yourself. A network is a charity in the true sense of the word, i.e., a love feast. It builds up you and others. Giving knowledge when asked and networking is pure service to others.

Quotations

"Why is it that people often do not know themselves very well (e.g., their own characters, why they feel the way they do, or even the feelings themselves)? And how can they increase their self-knowledge? … here's the problem: research on the adaptive unconscious suggests that much of what we want to see is unseeable. … The key is the kind of self-examination people perform, and the extent to which people attempt to know themselves solely by looking inward, versus looking outward at their own behavior and how others react to them."

—Timothy Wilson, Strangers to Ourselves *(pp. 3, 15–6)*

"There are risks … in maintaining illusions that are too out of whack. … there are times when it is to our benefit to pay close attention to what others think of us and to consider revising our self-views accordingly, even if this means adopting a more negative view of ourselves."

—Timothy Wilson, Strangers to Ourselves *(pp. 198-9)*

"Love is light is knowledge."

—The Cassiopaeans *(2 September 1995)*

PARABLES FOR
CONTEMPLATION

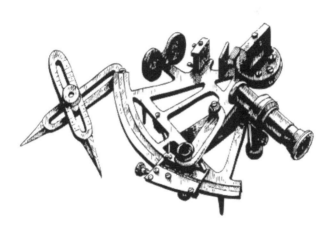

The Parable of the Coach

As long as man has not reached the point of fusion, his life will be in effect a factitious existence, as he himself will change from moment to moment. Since these changes will occur as a result of external shocks which he can almost never foresee, it will also be impossible for him to predict in advance the exact way he will change internally. Thus he will live subject to events as they occur, always preoccupied by constantly 'patching up' ('replastering'). He will in fact progress toward the unknown, at the mercy of chance. This state of things, named in the Tradition The Law of Chance, or *The Law of Accident*, is—for man as he is—the principal law under whose authority he leads his illusory existence.

Esoteric science indicates the possibilities and the means of freeing oneself from this law. It helps us to begin a new and purposeful life; first to become logical with ourselves, and finally, to become our own master.

But to begin effectively on this way, one must first clearly see the situation as it is. A parable found in the most ancient sources permits us to get a clear picture of this, and so keep this condition in mind. It is the parable of the *Coach*.

This image represents the characteristics of man by a coach. The physical body is represented by the coach itself; the horses represent sensations, feelings and passions; the coachman is the ensemble of the intellectual faculties including reason; the person

sitting in the coach is the master. In its normal state, the whole system is in a perfect state of operation: the coachman holds the reins firmly in his hands and drives the horses in the direction indicated by the master. This, however, is not how things happen in the immense majority of cases. First of all, the master is absent. The coach must go and find him, and must then await his pleasure. All is in a bad state: the axles are not greased and they grate; the wheels are badly fixed; the shaft dangles dangerously; the horses, although of noble race, are dirty and ill-fed; the harness is worn and the reins are not strong. The coachman is asleep: his hands have slipped to his knees and hardly hold the reins, which can fall from them at any moment.

The coach nevertheless continues to move forward, but does so in a way which presages no happiness. Abandoning the road, it is rolling down the slope in such a way that the coach is now pushing the horses, which are unable to hold it back. The coachman, fallen into a deep sleep, is swaying in his seat at risk of falling off. Obviously a sad fate awaits such a coach.

This image provides a highly appropriate analogy for the condition of most men, and it is worth taking as an object of meditation.

Salvation may however present itself. Another coachman, this one quite awake, may pass by the same route and observe the coach in its sad situation. If he is not much in a hurry, he may perhaps stop to help the coach that is in distress. He will first help the horses hold back the coach from slipping down the slope. Then he will awaken the sleeping driver and together with him will try to bring the coach back to the road. He will lend fodder and money. He might also give advice on the care of the horses, the address of an inn and a coach repairer, and indicate the proper route to follow.

It will be up to the assisted coachman afterward to profit, by his own efforts, from the help and the information received. It will be incumbent on him from this point on to put all things in order and, open eyed, to follow the path he had abandoned.

He will above all fight against sleep, for if he falls asleep again, and if the coach leaves the road again and again finds itself in the same danger, he cannot hope that chance will smile upon him a second time; that another coachman will pass at that moment and at that place and come to his aid once again.

—Boris Mouravieff, *Gnosis* (Vol. 1, pp. 3-4)

The Parable of the Doorkeeper

Watch therefore: for ye know not what hour your Lord doth come. But know this, that if the good-man of the house had known in what watch the thief would come, he would have watched, and would not have suffered his house to be broken up. Therefore be ye also ready: for in such an hour as ye think not the Son of man cometh. Who then is a faithful and wise servant, whom his lord hath made ruler over his household, to give them meat in due season?

Blessed is that servant, whom his lord when he cometh shall find so doing. Verily I say unto you, That he shall make him ruler over all his goods. But and if that evil servant shall say in his heart, My lord delayeth his coming; And shall begin to smite his fellow servants, and to eat and drink with the drunken; The lord of that servant shall come in a day when he looketh not for him, and in an hour that he is not aware of, And shall cut him asunder, and appoint him his portion with the hypocrites: there shall be weeping and gnashing of teeth.

—Matthew 24:42–51 (King James Version)

The Parable of the Prodigal Son

And he said, A certain man had two sons: And the younger of them said to his father, Father, give me the portion of goods that falleth to me. And he divided unto them his living. And not many days after the younger son gathered all together, and took his journey into a far country, and there wasted his substance with riotous living. And when he had spent all, there arose a mighty famine in that land; and he began to be in want. And he went and joined himself to a citizen of that country; and he sent him into his fields to feed swine.

And he would fain have filled his belly with the husks that the swine did eat: and no man gave unto him. And when he came to himself, he said, How many hired servants of my father's have bread enough and to spare, and I perish with hunger! I will arise and go to my father, and will say unto him, Father, I have sinned against heaven, and before thee, And am no more worthy to be called thy son: make me as one of thy hired servants.

And he arose, and came to his father. But when he was yet a great way off, his father saw him, and had compassion, and ran, and fell on his neck, and kissed him. And the son said unto him, Father, I have sinned against heaven, and in thy sight, and am no more worthy to be called thy son. But the father said to his servants, Bring forth the best robe, and put it on him; and put a ring on his hand, and shoes on his feet:

And bring hither the fatted calf, and kill it; and let us eat, and be merry: For this my son was dead, and is alive again; he was lost, and is found. And they began to be merry. Now his elder son was in the field: and as he came and drew nigh to the house, he heard musick and dancing. And he called one of the servants, and asked what these things meant. And he said unto him, Thy brother is come; and thy father hath killed the fatted calf, because he hath received him safe and sound. And he was angry, and would not go in: therefore came his father out, and intreated him.

And he answering said to his father, Lo, these many years do I serve thee, neither transgressed I at any time thy commandment: and yet thou never gavest me a kid, that I might make merry with my friends:

But as soon as this thy son was come, which hath devoured thy living with harlots, thou hast killed for him the fatted calf. And he said unto him, Son, thou art ever with me, and all that I have is thine. It was meet that we should make merry, and be glad: for this thy brother was dead, and is alive again; and was lost, and is found.

—Luke 15:11–13 (King James Version)

EXPANDED GLOSSARY AND DEFINITIONS

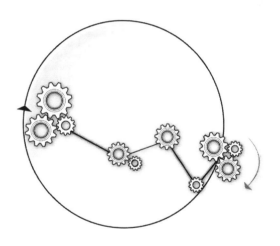

Anticipation and non-Anticipation

The Cassiopaea material discusses anticipation in relation to following one's path or interacting with reality at large. There two sides to the discussion; the first being that one should always anticipate attack in order to avoid problems by preparation; the second is that one should not be fixated on any particular imagined outcome of one's creative efforts because such fixation or anticipation restricts the 'creative flow.'

This is the closest the Cassiopaeans come to discussing 'you create your own reality' or 'YCYOR.'

Intent can invite realization but anticipation of any particular realization metaphysically nullifies the intent. Anticipation is expecting the self to be confirmed, expecting to bend the universe to one's will and thus falls on the side of the service to self principle. Intent is non-personal and can be generally creative in the service to others sense. Anticipation does however have its uses in a world of service to self but this use is for the service to others candidate principally in predicting and blocking possible foreseeable difficulties. This takes the form of simple physical or mental preparedness.

An alternative formulation of the idea could be that if one thinks one must have more money, the idea of having more money is projected into the future and the idea of not having enough money is asserted for the present. In the reverse, if one thinks one could get mugged and therefore avoids the side alley after dark, one asserts that one could be mugged in the future and is safe in the present and to give this idea physical expression even avoids places where muggings are the most common. If any part of mind really influences reality by metaphysically attracting events, it is not the conscious wishing part. If this part has effect on reality, the effect is rather in selecting what is an appropriate perception, hence blocking much information that would otherwise be available. This too has a survival oriented role but it is over-expressed in people who will only accept that which conforms to their assumptions or anticipations.

Another way of thinking about this would be the idea that ignoring something is an invitation for experientially learning this something. This is generally so in the case of ignoring warnings of impending danger. The 'all giving universe' responds by allowing one to experience the danger.

We could say that uses of anticipation are defensive and rooted in knowledge of possible dangers. Anticipation can also be used in a controlling sense when people make precise plans about carrying out a project that has little to do with openness to the 'creative principle.' Such activity is mostly concerned with meeting external requirements or getting confirmation for oneself being in control.

Having internal discipline is a somewhat different matter. Discipline implies staying the course and being consistent, while not "anticipating" specific outside effects as a result of merely expecting them.

The greatest creative contribution in the service to others mode can be realized in a state of not anticipating outcomes or effects while expressing one's fundamental nature or gift. Much work may be required to properly know this gift and where its use is appropriate. It is not a simple process of self-expression, as it includes doing this in accordance with objective reality. Openness to reality is what makes constructive and non-restricting response possible. Without this objectivity and state of non-assumption one is again forcing one's interpretation, even if unconsciously, on reality.

Acting completely on behalf of universal principles and on an unbiased seeing of reality without any desire for the self is vanishingly rare. Still, combining intent with accurate perception can lead one to entirely unexpected openings and synchronicities. Placing too many restrictions on what are acceptable openings may simply lead one to miss them. This is more a manifestation of obsession than objective seeing.

This idea is tied to the adage that knowledge protects. Knowledge of risks makes preparing for them possible and may offer some psychic protection also. Obsession with specific results is not knowledge, it imposes one's subjectivity on the world and thus does not protect, but can invite quite the contrary. Thus flexibility and objective perception are key.

Laura Knight-Jadczyk, *The Wave*, Chapter 23 (excerpt)

What is wrong with efforts to send love and light, the achieving of the goals of world peace or personal prosperity? What is wrong with wanting a return to God, or higher consciousness or any of the touted experiences that are guaranteed to initiate a person to whatever they desire? The problem is *anticipation*. When you seek any of these things by holding the thoughts in the left-brain in anticipation of making it real, you are raping the maiden of the well.

What if you are just trying to believe it is now? Belief is a function of the left brain; it blocks the manifestation of creativity because the creative right brain is also the empirical half of the brain that observes the dichotomy between the belief and the reality.

Desire is anticipation. Anticipation is read by the right brain as in the future, therefore not right now, and the right brain can only create now. When we desire, we have a future object in mind. The right brain only knows now.

If we desire to love God, we have a concept (left brain) of the future goal of loving God. It can't exist now. Therefore we experience struggle to constantly love God, against the ongoing now of not loving God.

If we desire to win the lottery, and produce in the left brain future image of money flowing into our life, it isn't now. So now continues moneyless.

If we desire happiness, and create the concept in the left brain, we have future happiness in mind. And the right brain reads it as unhappiness now, and this can manifest in thousands of unhappy experiences.

By the same token, if we send love and light to any directed recipient, we are holding a concept of future fixing that signals a state of brokenness now to our right brain, and the repercussions are felt in our life. In a larger sense, we may be signaling the collective right brain that a future state of peace is desired, and therefore, now is not peaceful. And so the right brain creates now. The perception of linear time constantly projects rewards into the future, blocking access to the present, like a donkey chasing a carrot for all eternity.

> Q: (L) If someone wanted to win the lottery, for example, what would be the correct approach? What should they do, or be, or think, or say?
> A: Completely pure intent, i.e., open. Nonanticipatory.
> Q: (L) Anticipation constricts the channels of creativity?
> A: Yes.
> Q: (L) A person has to be completely uncaring whether they get it or not, so to speak?

A: Happy-go-lucky attitude helps.

Q: (L) So, worry, tension, anticipation, and attachment to the idea, we constricts the flow?

A: Yes.

But you noticed, I hope, that intent is not considered to be anticipation or desire. The words themselves may provide a clue.

Anticipate: *ante*—before + *capare*—to take. To look forward to; to expect; to make happen earlier, precipitate; to foresee and perform in advance, etc.

We see clearly the connection between anticipation and time.

Intent: firmly directed or fixed; having the mind or attention firmly directed or fixed; engrossed; strongly resolved; a purpose or objective; will and determination at the time of performing an act.

Do we see a subtle difference? Even if it is somewhat semantically, it is sufficient to make us think about how to deal with our creative potential.

Of course, we see that completely pure intent is a pretty tall order. Thus we see that the key becomes acting now with intent, but no imaginary anticipation for the future. A goal, with applied *will* of action, which necessitates left brain conscious preparing and planning, via the heightened awareness of the right brain, which deals directly with the present conditions, will result in an opening of life changing creative potential.

Q: (L) Okay, we've been talking earlier this evening about intent, and of course, our own experiences with intent have really been pretty phenomenal. We've come to some kind of an idea that intent, when confirmed repeatedly, actually builds force. Is this a correct concept, and is there anything that you can add to it?

A: Only until anticipation muddies the picture … tricky one, huh?

Q: (L) Is anticipation the act of assuming you know how something is going to happen?

A: Follows realization, generally, and unfortunately for you, on 3rd density. You see, once anticipation enters the picture, the intent can no longer be STO.

Q: (L) Anticipation is desire for something for self. Is that it?

A: Yes.

Q: (L) Okay, so it's okay to intend something, or to think in an intentional way, or to hope in an intentional way, for something that is to serve another …

A: And that brings realization. But, realization creates anticipation.

Q: (L) Well, how do we navigate this razor? I mean, this is like walking on a razor's edge. To control your mind to not anticipate, and yet, deal with realization, and yet, still maintain hope …

A: Mental exercises of denial, balanced with pure faith of a non-prejudicial kind.

Q: (L) Okay, so, in other words, to just accept what is at the moment, appreciate it as it is at the moment, and have faith that the universe and things will happen the way they are supposed to happen, without placing any expectation on how that will be, and keep on working?

A: Yes.

Q: (L) We have discussed a lot of concepts about shaping the future. In our discussions, we have hypothesized that it is something like an intentional act of shaping something good, but without defining the moment of measurement. In other words, adding energy to it by intent, but not deciding where, when or how the moment of measurement occurs. Like a quantum jump: you know it is statistically likely, but not definite, so you cannot expect it, but you observe so that you can notice when it occurs on it's own, and in it's own way.

A: Yes. Avoiding anticipation. That is the key to shaping the future … When it hits you, it stops.

Q: (L) When what hits you? The fact that it's happening? That you are doing it?

A: Yes unless you cancel out all anticipation.

Q: (L) Well, this is very tricky.

A: Ah? We have doubts … And yes, you create your own reality!

Q: (L) Well, but you have also said that anticipation messes things up, and so I don't want to have any anticipation.

A: Anticipation is not creating one's own reality.

If *non*-anticipation opens the door to the creativity of the universe, what closes the door to negative occurrences? Can it be that we have a clue here as well?

Just remember that anticipation is the "mother of preparation", and defense.

Lesson number 1: always expect attack.
Lesson number 2: know the modes of same.
Lesson number 3: know how to counteract same.

When you are under attack, expect the unexpected, if it is going to cause problems … But, if you expect it, you learn how to "head it off", thus neutralizing it. This is called vigilance, which is rooted in knowledge. Knowledge protects. (The Cassiopaeans)

So, it seems that the answer to this part of the problem is that when we are connected to the Cosmos via the right brain, and are not blocking the ability of our Cosmic Connection by limiting the forces with boundary forming imagination or images or illusory concepts, we allow the perfect manifestation of our own frequency resonance to occur. By the same token, when necessary, we can close the door to manipulation of our minds by constantly running a sort of computer scan of possible breaches of our security system in the left brain. We must marry the left brain kingship of the material world to the right brain queen of the inner realm.

Yet, it was only when Parzival rejected *all* of the advice, the exhortations, when he quit seeking to be a great knight on a sacred quest to save the world; only when he rejected God as the pure and good all-father that ... it found him.

What is the wasteland? That we cannot accept the world and all within it, including ourselves, as being perfectly natural and perfect just the way it is—with all the good and evil it contains as part of the natural and necessary balance—the whole of existence is natural and as it should be at every moment. When you accept that all is perfect, when you cease holding God hostage by usurping the power of the right brain feminine principle with the images in your left brain, then the world will be perfect and fertile and you will heal the wound of the wasteland in your own heart.

If only we can act spontaneously, without being programmed into someone else's belief system, we can ask the real question of ourselves; ask with no preconceived notion of what the answer will be; ask with no anticipation.

Then, miraculously, for one moment the vessel of the Grail is empty … and in the next it is filled with the wonder and glory of *all* and everything.

> The Spirit of the Valley never dies. It is called the Mystic Female. The Door of the Mystic Female is the root of Heaven and Earth. (Lao Tzu)

And the Mystic Female is the infinite Sea of potential. It is God in the *not* aspect that only can be when expectations, anticipations, assumptions and obsessions are completely left at the door.

> Negative existence is the silence behind the sound, the blank canvas beneath the painting, the darkness into which light shines. Emptiness is the stillness against which time moves. Negative existence enables a man to be what he is. It is the mirror of mirrors. Non-anticipation is noninterference, and allows the most perfect reflection of creation. (Lao Tzu)

The Cassiopaean Experiment

This is the name of a channeled source contacted by Laura Knight-Jadczyk for the first time in 1994. Diverse other people have participated in the channeling process, most often through a OUIJA board, but Knight-Jadczyk is the only constant participant and primus motor. The Cassiopaeans identify themselves as 'you in the future' and as '6th density light beings.' According to the source, the 'you' refers to a number of people who 'recognize the application' of the information imparted by the channeled source and the research for which this information has been an inspiration.

Quantum entanglement displays superluminal communication but cannot be used for information transfer. When the state of one of the entangled particles is measured, the other entangled particle turns out the same. This does not transmit information between measurement points. Transmitting information from the future to the past violates causality because the past which is the prerequisite for the future's existence is modified by the information. This need not be an absolute barrier for superluminal communication if the communication is inherently noisy or probabilistic in nature.

The channeling phenomenon is one possible instance of superluminal communication directly received by a consciousness. It is however undemonstrable as a process as understood by modern physics. Such communication forms paradoxes only if the world were interpreted as deterministic. In the QFS's thinking, superluminal communication between past and future selves is a probabilistic phenomenon which ties certain possible pasts to certain possible futures by means of a sort of feedback loop. However, all superluminal communication need not come from the same possible future.

Many years of research, experience, and constructive curiosity led to Laura's experiment in superluminal communication that eventually, after two years of experimentation and fine-tuning, resulted in the Cassiopaean Transmissions. Ever since then the process has been refined and all "instruments" adjusted for higher accuracy and facilitation of better communication. These communications are different from most other channeled information. It is "critical channeling" that discourages blind devotee-ism. The Cassiopeans themselves do not demand to be worshipped or deified in any way and, in fact, admonish against such an attitude toward them. They encourage researching and networking with others to verify the information they transmit and do not demand that anything be taken at face value without questions.

The Cassiopaea material is somewhat different in style and content from other material received from allegedly similar sources, such as Ra or the Pleiadians. The metaphysical or cosmological discourse is quite compatible with the aforementioned but the Cassiopaea material is more specific and hands-on. Of contemporary channeled sources, Cassiopaea is unique in that there the channeled material has been the starting point, not the end product. The fact that Knight-Jadczyk and her associates have extensively researched the field covered by the channeled material and used this research for formulating further avenues of inquiry lends a unique hands-on, interactive tone to the material. Cassiopaea contains almost no vague, generic lectures on metaphysics, as are commonly found with channeled material. For a somewhat systematic exploration of the cosmology on which Cassiopaea develops further, one can see Ra.

The principal themes covered are:

- Man's possibility for spiritual progress through understanding and dealing with dynamics of daily life.
- Present day secret government, alien related and conspiracy material. This is explored in general and also as relates to the authors' personal experience.
- History, ancient as well as modern. In ancient history, lost civilizations such as Atlantis and former cataclysms and alien participation in human evolution and manipulation thereof are discussed.
- Directions of research for physics, indirectly dealing with themes such as gravity, spacetime manipulation, densities, UFT.

- Material on probable future events, most importantly the Wave, a possible point of transition between densities, possibly allowing the 'graduation' of a portion of humanity to 4th density. The 'lessons of 3rd density' are discussed in this context.

The information received from this experiment is presented in the context of broad-ranging historical, scientific and metaphysical material and offers clues that have led to the worldview and inferences presented in our numerous publications on this website and in print. Perhaps it is only our subconscious that presents itself as a "source" but even so, does that tell us something more? Do we really know what the unconscious mind is and what it is capable of?

The core of the practical advice given by the Cassiopaea source consists of networking, study and developing objectivity. Only by learning the lessons at hand can one advance. There are notable parallels between Cassiopaeans and other esoteric teachings, notably Sufism and the 4th Way. The Cassiopaea material has been brought to a larger context of esoteric teachings drawing on many sources and streams by Laura Knight-Jadczyk. Thus the teaching of the QFS is not exclusively based on the Cassiopaea material although this is its initial impulse and platform.

External and Internal Considering

In 4th Way parlance, this is the practice of taking others into account when acting. External considering involves making a realistic evaluation of another's situation and acting in ways which take this into account in a positive sense.

External considering is however not the same thing as being

socially polite or considerate, although it may be expressed in this manner.

The key concept is to be aware of and to adapt oneself to the level of being and knowledge of others. Thus, external considering involves for example not talking about things which would simply offend others' beliefs or simply not be understood. External considering relates to an idea of general good will towards the environment, then in the sense of letting the environment be as it wishes and responding to its requests in a manner that honors its right to be as it will.

External considering is rooted in objective awareness of the environment. Its opposite, internal considering, is rooted in attachment to a subjective inner state, to one's own comfort of preconceptions or desires.

External and internal considering are not always outwardly distinguishable, although inwardly they are fundamentally different. One may for example be socially pleasing purely in order to reinforce one's own idea of oneself as a 'good person.' This is internal considering and preoccupation about how others/the self perceive the self.

In some cases, external considering may involve withholding information that is seen as inappropriate, dangerous or simply unlikely to be well received. An internally considering person may also do this, but then again the motive is different.

We cannot codify with external criteria which action constitutes which kind of considering. The concepts are related to service to others vs. service to self and to objectivity vs. subjectivity. Usually the term considering is applied in the context of personal interactions.

Only through having external considering can one serve others. This requires responsiveness and a sense of objectivity and awareness of what is right action for the given situation. Serving in the sense of merely carrying out commands is not external considering.

Internal considering can be likened to man's inner predator. It feeds itself by engaging in subjective fantasies where it thinks it is other than it is. It will also seek to gain external confirmation for its distorted self-image by manipulating others to confirm it in its views. Man may go to much trouble to make an impression, simply in order to have his own illusory, internally considered self-image reflected back to himself from others. All success in such manipulation feeds the predator and confirms it in its internal considering and accordingly removes the center of gravity of man's inner life away from objectivity. Internal considering is in very concrete terms man's natural enemy who seeks to prevent man from being himself. The predator will at all times prefer an illusion of virtue to the naked truth about itself. Still, it is not useful to morally judge or condemn the predator, just like it is useless to condemn a cat for eating mice. Still, one must disengage from identifying with this predator. Claiming to Work while engaging in internal considering is a contradiction in terms. The forms of internal considering can however be extremely subtle and one cannot always detect them, thus constant vigilance is required. The predator of internal considering may well claim to engage in merciless self-observation, to aspire to consciousness and being and any other virtues and even trick itself to believe it is progressing towards these goals while all the while only feeding its vanity and desire for recognition.

Exterior man needs the support of a group in order to help him detect the many tricky ways in which internal considering inserts itself in his perception and actions.

Networking

Whereas self-serving beings naturally form hierarchies with the strongest and most ruthless at the top, service to others beings would form networks. In the words of the Cassiopaeans, the concept of networking is a foretaste of 4th density STO.

To bring the idea into context, we can start with Gurdjieff's definition of a group: In a group, what is gained by one is gained by all and what is lost by one is lost by all. A group in this sense can only exist within the context of esoteric work. Such a group is free from disagreement not because of a command structure but because the same truths are seen by all. See the article on Esoteric, Mesoteric and Exoteric circles for more.

We can distinguish two types of group effects: The first is where the group descends to the level of the lowest common denominator, as happens in lynch mobs and other cases of mass hysteria. We can envision a situation where the whole group would rise to the sum total of the understandings and capacities of all members. The latter happens to a small degree in teams displaying good synergy. However, the imperfect quality of human communication and friction coming from personality dampens these effects and usually limits their scope to a well-practised area such as playing a team sport or playing in an orchestra.

The hope of esoteric work is to make these effects greater and more comprehensive. Achieving this is sometimes called the communion of saints. This goes beyond a social phenomenon and involves sharing the 'substance of knowledge' or 'higher hydrogens' generated in group work.

In general we can say that a group amplifies whatever is a consistently shared and applied principle in the group's work. This contains a catch: We often find, specially on the Internet,

New Age groups that are in a sense 'open' but where the exchange degenerates if not into a shouting match then into a more subtle feeding or pleading or manipulating contest. It seems that internal work for purifying the signal and making the self first clear is a prerequisite for a group to amplify anything but subjectivity. For mixed, predominantly self-serving entities such as present day humans, indiscriminate sharing of everything simply makes noise. A great deal of attention is required for the participants to overcome first themselves and then act in a manner approximating STO oriented beings, thus not according to their default impulses. Again, determining what constitutes service to others in which case is its own question but a certain skill or sense for this can form via practice.

In practice, a network does not imply the interchangeability of all members. This is not achievable nor is it the goal. Having reached a similar level of development does not imply identity of personality or group think but does imply striving for seeing the same understandings. A group can involve specialization and contain teachers and students but is by definition a voluntary structure and does not exist for the benefit of any single member or subgroup. Instead, such a group may exist for performing a specific esoteric task, as may be required by the time and context.

The concept of giving back is emphasized by the 4th Way. Since the principle of service to others represents balance through the idea of serving self through serving others, this principle requires reciprocity in order to work. Balance cannot be legislated but it may occur naturally if the participants share the same direction, i.e. are collinear.

For 4th density harvestability, a network offers distinct advantages over working alone. The members can complete each other even though their own vibrational purity were not perfect.

For graduating to 4th density STS, the aspirants must generally work alone since the very idea of service to self sees sharing as generally undesirable.

Paleo Diet Summary

Anti-inflammatory

- foods which stimulate the immune system as little as possible
- allows the gut to repair its tight-junction leaks and microvilli damage from gluten, casein, etc.
- no sugar, grains, dairy, starch, legumes, nightshades, vegetable oils/trans fats and insoluble fiber
- some foods may be reintroduced in limited amounts once the gut has been repaired (do elimination testing)

Ketogenic

- no more than 50 g carbs/day (often far less, and zero for those more sensitive)
- 80% of calories from animal fats (do not fear saturate fat or cholesterol)
- no more than 0.9-1.2 g protein per kg of body weight
- no more than 25 g protein per serving, to reduce mTOR activity (approx. 3.5 oz meat/egg per serving)
- increase protein intake depending on exercise requirements, repairing injuries, etc.
- bone broth and organ meats are super-foods

Micronutrients

- Vit-C is a potent antioxidant, antimicrobial, and anti-cancer agent

- liposomal or IV delivery is optimal
- Magnesium is a common deficiency due to depleted agricultural soils
- Epsom salt baths are a potent delivery mechanism for absorption
- Iron overload
    - iron can reach dangerous levels in some individuals on high-meat diets
    - test serum iron, ferritin, and transferrin after being in ketosis for a while
    - phlebotomy or chelation with DMSA or EDTA are viable detox strategies

Sourcing

- organic, antibiotic- and pesticide-free, non-GMO foods as much as possible
- avoid animals fed or finished on grains
- free range, pasture-raised animals are healthiest and most ethical

Eating/Lifestyle habits

- your last meal should be >3 hours before bed
- chewing your food thoroughly (~20 bites) increases nutrient absorption
- having dimmer lights and less electronic stimulation can reduce appetite
- resistance exercise to stimulate mitochondria growth and function

A simple plan for integrating dietary changes in your life:

Step one, day 1: Remove all gluten from your diet. All grains contain some amounts of gluten. The worst is wheat and the least bad is rice. So you can keep rice for a period of transition, say 10 days. After 10 days, ALL grains should be eliminated totally. Not even so-called "gluten-free" breads are safe. This is hard, of course, but you can fill the gap by eating more vegetables and meats. Eat your vegetables with plenty of real butter on them (no additives). Eat meats with fat on them and eat the fat. This is an essential part of the cure. Start your day with bacon and eggs or ham and eggs and eat all you want.

Do this for TEN DAYS and then move to step two.

Step two, day 11: After 10 days, cut out rice and all beans (except green beans) completely. You should now be having no grains at all, in any form, in your diet. Read labels on everything. If there is a single word pertaining to a grain product, do NOT eat it. Continue to eat plenty of vegetables and meats with all the fat and added butter. Do not use cooking sprays. Instead, cook with duck fat or lard.

Do this additional step for the next TEN DAYS. Then move to step three.

Step three, day 21: Remove all sugars from the diet. This includes all fruits. Do not replace this with any foods containing artificial sweeteners because they are excitotoxins and cause great harm. The only sweeteners allowed are xylitol, sorbitol, or stevia. No honey, no corn syrup, NO forms of sugar at all. You can drink tea or coffee with xylitol and that will help with cravings. Increase your fat intake. The fat on beef, pork, or duck is good. You can continue to eat most vegetables. (Make sure that you use only olive oil and vinegar on salads; no commercial dressings.)

Do this additional step for TEN DAYS.

Step four, day 31: Remove all dairy products except butter from the diet. All nuts, too. At this point, you will be eating only meat and vegetables. You should eat more cooked vegetables than raw (salad), and eat them with plenty of butter.

We've left dairy to this point because it can sometimes ease the issues that removing gluten creates.

Step five, day 41: Stop coffee; you can have green or black or mint teas. Gradually reduce the quantity of vegetables that you eat and fill the gap with meat and meat fats. This means that if you eat a piece of meat, it should have almost as much fat on it as lean. You can eat as much meat as you want, but be sparing with vegetables, giving preference to cooked ones over raw.

For more information, visit the Health section of the Cassiopaea Forum.

Recapitulation

This is a technique of inner work described by Castaneda. Recapitulation involves making a list of all persons with whom one has interacted throughout one's life and remembering in vivid detail any places one has been to, situations one has experienced and so forth. This may involve traveling to places, keeping a journal of memories, written notes etc.

The idea of recapitulation is to free oneself from one's past through bringing it to consciousness. This is similar to the idea of modern psychotherapy but recapitulation is primarily to be done as a private exercise.

Recapitulation seeks to integrate all aspects of memory, a bit like self-remembering seeks to integrate all aspects of a present moment. The technique stimulates memory and associations and may offer interesting material for self-observation in the form of discovering surprising networks of apparently unrelated associations.

As with such techniques in general, effects are liable to vary greatly between individuals.

Self-Remembering

This is the 4th Way practice of dividing attention. Normally, one is in a state of constantly shifting identification. Self-remembering can be used to break this automation.

In its basic form, the practice involves being aware of one's inner state, including body, emotions and thinking, while also paying attention to an external object or activity. Self-remembering can bring presence of consciousness into human activity which usually is mechanical and simply happens.

Self-remembering is a prerequisite of self-knowledge and work on the self. Self-remembering is not simply analysis of self based on past data. It is by definition an activity that takes place in the present and concerns the present. It is not for example 'recapitulation,' which concerns the past.

A simple exercise of self-remembering is becoming conscious of one's body, emotion and thought and then alternatingly look at objects, while holding all these present to one's attention. One notices that one very easily falls into identification, where attention is drawn to a single object from its divided state.

Self-remembering in the middle of emotional shocks is specially difficult but also very valuable to the Work. Repeated practice of this goes in the direction of forming a constant I which is less and less subject to being captured into identification with passing circumstance. This is essential for forming cohesive being, intent and eventually capacity to 'do' in the 4th Way meaning of the term.

Another aspect of the concept relates to man's physical and psychic metabolism. Man takes in three kinds of 'food:' physical food, air and impressions. These three 'substances,' also known in the Work as 'hydrogens' undergo change and refinement in the human being. This goes in the direction of more refined, less coarse, more vivifying substances, ones more infused with information and intelligence, if one can say so. This process usually happens only very partially and the human 'hydrogen factory' is leaky and inefficient. Self-remembering, specially when done in context of shocks, assists and energizes these processes, so that finer hydrogens can be produced in greater quantity. This may have the effect of connecting one to one's higher centers. In this sense, self-remembering goes beyond a means of intellectually knowing about the self and becomes a tool for transformation and unlocking qualitatively new possibilities.

Intense self-remembering can happen spontaneously in situations of great emotional shock or danger. One observes then an entirely different quality of perception and presence. At such moments, the organism is prompted to work in a different mode, producing a momentary flow of 'higher hydrogens,' which enable a different type of functioning. The Work seeks to make these states available in a predictable and systematic fashion.

Strategic Enclosure

Those who are familiar with the Parable of the Prodigal Son can understand that the realization alone that one is "in the pigsty of the foreign country" would serve to produce the state of alert, the condition for the "journey home." This is crucial since, in the story of the Prodigal son, we also see that when the son went to the "resident of the foreign land" to ask for help, he was sent to live and feed with the pigs. This exemplifies that principle that the Radiant being must understand at all times that the Lords of Entropy—the Powers That Be in this reality—will always try to reclaim them as servants. Additionally, belief in the ownership of the land, belief in "being at home" in this world, or being "in charge" of this world, can give a false sense of security to the Radiant being leading them to lower their guard and succumb to the Power of Illusion.

With this in mind, the Radiant being should then create an "Enclosure" around their "being."

The forces of entropy which govern this reality at present, are much stronger than the powers of resistance of the individual Radiant being. This fact leads us to consider the principle of the enclosure as a psychological policy, in relation to ourselves and to the exterior world, which will allow us to compensate for our lack of strength and available reserves by an appropriate strategy.

Because of millennia of cultural and religious conditioning, everything about us is limited, beginning with our nervous resistance. The rule which can be deduced from this is that we must—as much as possible—work silently so as not to draw increased attention and pressure upon ourselves while working on the process of awakening and assimilating knowledge and interior force that can restore us to the Edenic condition. This is true for the average Radiant being, because if he attracts the attention of what Mouravieff calls the General Law that mechanically rules this reality, he will be lost, as the reaction of the 'World' against him will be extreme.

What the Radiant being must do is to consciously master the material that is part of his interior world—his Belief Centers—by gaining sufficient knowledge to be able to exercise perspicacity and SEEing. This enables him to divide that which he perceives and to choose that which is assimilated, or "enters within" his "strategic enclosure." This allows him to accumulate force and put it in reserve. When the false beliefs, the illusions of this world, no longer have any part within the Radiant Being, then he will be able to step out of the flow of Linear Time.

The principle of the strategic enclosure is, then, that the individual or group must initially work silently to create this enclosure, without drawing the attention of the forces of life of this world to himself. These forces are systematically hostile to anyone who persistently searches for the Truth.

There are two parts to the Strategic Enclosure: The first is to shelter oneself physically from the harmful influence of the 'World' as much as possible. Gurdjieff referred to this as the activity of the "sly man." Unfortunately, this has often been twisted to mean the "monastic life" or "withdrawal from the world" which is an essentially useless approach when the thing that needs most to be learned is the objective truth of the reality in which we live.

The second part of the Strategic Enclosure is that the shelter must be built in his inner world. Mouravieff writes that "The picturesque language of the Tradition says that man must build a cage in himself. This must be provided with all means of connection with and direction of the centres. It must also be solid enough to effectively resist all rebellions of the little 'I's, singly or 'federated'. This construction takes time. To play its role as an organ of direction, it must be continually enlarged, improved and perfected."

In other words, the Strategic Enclosure is an allegory that refers to an ontological state where the individual basically declares his independence from the Law of Entropy that seems to govern the Material Universe. Using the concepts explained by Mouravieff, this state could also be described as a manifestation of a resolution to shut oneself up to the influences of illusion and instead open only to those influences that lead one to objectivity.

The Creative Hyperdimensional Wisdom claimed that once having "enclosed the land occupied," the people then could cultivate it and make it produce fruits. This, again, must be understood allegorically ——even if the end result may be quite material. This is also reflected in alchemical metaphors as well as in one of the most famous examples given by Jesus: the miracle of the loaves and fishes which is merely an example of the fact that Jesus was a master of the Creative Hyperdimensional Wisdom which had expressed this principle in many other allegories including that of the Head of Bran and the Cauldron of Regeneration.

The principle of the Strategic Wall is, in its more immediate meaning, the practical application of the principle of Enclosure, however the fact that there are different manifestations of this strategic wall depending on the realm to which it is applied is made clear by the fact that there are many worlds where the Spirit remains captive and in each one of them the principle of the Strategic Wall supposes a different manifestation.

It could be said that, in the physical world the correct application might lead to construction of a Stone Wall, but one must understand that the definition of a "Stone Wall", as manifested in the physical realm, should not be constricted to the idea of a *spatially closed wall*. There are obviously many principles that belong to "Lithic Wisdom", which suggest that that a "stone wall" is related to the emplacement of megaliths in very specific layouts for the purpose of creating a grid that may have served, as one of its purposes, to protect the enclosed space from the influence of the Entropic Principle.

The Strategic Enclosure, then, aims at the innermost part of each man, creating a space in which awakening can take place. This awakening calls to them, and through their blood connections it calls to all others who are of the Radiant lineage, to cease their march along the "evolutionary" or "progressive" path of History and to rebel against the Laws of Entropy that reduce all to primal matter. Awakening induces the Radiant ones to take a leap in the opposite direction and transmute man's "animal tendencies" [the reactive machine programs of Gurdjieff, the Predator of Don Juan, the confluence with the General Law of Mouravieff] and claim back their divine Hyperdimensional nature.

To achieve this latter Racial purpose, as opposed to the individual one, do have the help of an "external element".

What, specifically, is this "external element"?

It's the one thing whose sole description would fill entire volumes and which is often referred to as the Grail.

The Wave

In the Cassiopaea material this is a cyclic cosmic event, slated to next take place on Earth and its environment in the near future. This is variously referred to as the transition to 4th density, shift of the ages, harvest and by many other terms in many bodies of material.

The idea of a cosmic event taking place in the early 21st century has been seeping into increasingly general circulation ever since the late 19th century. Gurdjieff, for instance, makes veiled references to such a thing when speaking of a time allotted for certain preparation to take place on Earth. Theosophists and Steiner also allude to such a thing.

The Ra material (Law of One), from the early 1980's speaks

of such an event in more detail, introducing the idea of a 'planetary transition to 4th density.' The Cassiopaea material, since 1994, picks up on the theme left by Ra and discusses the transition in more specifics.

The QFS sees the Wave as a strong working hypothesis but does not claim to possess certainty on its validity or a formal definition of the concept.

The QFS interpretation of the concept could be outlined as follows: The universe involves different levels of being, each inhabited by entities suited to the level. Some of these levels are in part physical, such as the one which present day humanity inhabits. Natural processes cause the veil between these levels to periodically be thinned or breached, creating a sort of crossroads or conduit. This is a sort of superposition of many usually sealed levels of being.

Outside of the natural process, there are entities which use technology or psychic capabilities for passing between levels. The UFO phenomenon is one example of this. These levels are called densities in the C and Ra materials. Other sources use other names, such as cosmoses in the 4th Way literature.

The degree of development of a consciousness determines which level of density is natural to it. For certain esoterically developed humans, their level of being approaches the level required for inhabiting the 4th density, a level of being with a radically different perception of space, time and physicality. The natural circumstance of the Wave, i.e. the narrowing of the natural gap between levels of density thus offers a possibility of passage to those that are ready. Hence the term graduation or ascension. Polarization to either service to others (STO) or service to self (STS) is usually seen as the central requirement for the passage.

This ties to the 4th Way teaching in the sense that man must become a single, unambiguous entity before such a polarization even makes sense. Thus the 4th Way work on the self is necessary in order to create a self that is solid and consistent enough to bridge the transition between densities.

The Wave is seen as a point of turbulence. The arrival of the Wave is seen as coinciding with various cataclysmic upheavals, both in terms of society and nature.

The Wave has been compared to a waterfall. The river runs placidly up to the brink, then plunges down as a very turbulent stream and again settles into a riverbed of relative stability. A swimmer cannot escape the river but may make adjustments of course for avoiding rocks at the bottom of the plunge if he is aware of these. Also possibilities of a phase change, i.e. evaporation are greater in the cloud of spray surrounding the fall.

Phase change, as in passage from solid to liquid to gaseous has been used as an analogy for shift of density. A small increment of energy causes qualitative changes in the substance and its properties.

In the waterfall analogy, we note that in order to survive the plunge, one must be solid. When applied to a group of beings, as well as to the multiple little I's of each individual, this means that these must be cohesive and aligned to a common purpose. The QFS uses the term colinearity for this when speaking of a group. When speaking of an individual the term is fusion or having a real I. Failing this quality, one is likely to be ripped apart by the turbulence and not to preserve recognizable existence.

The QFS suggests that in the specific volatile circumstances corresponding to the waterfall, the quality of observation contributed to the process by the participants may make a large change in the outcome. This outcome may involve passage between densities, for example. Another example may be a split in timelines, as in the many worlds interpretation of quantum physics. Thus persons embracing one mode of being may literally end up in a different reality than other persons.

The processes in question are not strictly physical, although physical chaos is one likely reflection of the wider process. The process is seen as a macrocosmic quantum jump, determined by conscious observation. Just like the observation event is needed to force a quantum system to a specific state, observation is needed to guide the events inside the Wave.

This is one reason for the QFS's and 4th Way Work's emphasis on objectivity and clarity of understanding and work on forging a real I.

Polarization to a sufficient purity of STS or STO is not possible without knowledge of the world and a capacity for long term, unambiguous work. Still further, a group is needed to bring the requisite scope and consistency to the observation.

Failing to achieve a critical mass of STO-oriented consciousness in time for the Wave will likely cause the planet as a whole to remain in the hands of the present STS-oriented control system, divided in a 3rd density and 4th density group, the latter feeding on the former, as has been the case throughout history. Essentially, this amounts to a re-run of Earth history, from the dawn of man up to present, until the next cyclic coming of the Wave. According to the Cassiopaeans, the period of the cycle is about 309,000 years.

RECOMMENDED READING

Self-Work

Laura Knight-Jadczyk, *The Wave or Adventures with Cassiopaea* (Vols. 1–8).
Boris Mouravieff, *Gnosis* (Vols. 1–3).
P. D. Ouspensky, *In Search of the Miraculous*.

Emotional & Physical Health

Peter Levine, *In An Unspoken Voice*.
Nora Gedgaudas, *Primal Body, Primal Mind*.
Christian B. Allan & Wolfgang Lutz, *Life Without Bread*.
Lierre Keith, *The Vegetarian Myth*.

Psychology

Timothy Wilson, *Strangers to Ourselves*.
Martha Stout, *The Myth of Sanity*.
Stephanie Donaldson-Pressman and Robert M. Pressman, *The Narcissistic Family*.
Andrew Lobaczewski, *Political Ponerology*.

History

Laura Knight-Jadczyk, *The Secret History of the World* (Vols. 1-2).

Websites

www.cassiopedia.org
www.cassiopaea.org
www.eiriu-eolas.org
www.sott.net

For an extended list of recommended books, see the Cassiopaea Forum: www.cassiopaea.org/forum/index.php?topic=4718

NOTES

NOTES

Made in the USA
San Bernardino, CA
16 December 2013